CONTENTS

INTRODUCTION

When George Washington became president in 1789, no one knew how to address him. Some said that Washington's title should be "His Elective Majesty." Others wanted to call him "His Highness, the President of the United States and Protector of the Rights of the Same." Finally, agreement was reached. Washington was known as "President of the United States."

How was the new president to act? Should citizens bow to him? What would his powers be? George Washington helped develop the role of president. Forty-one other men have followed him and each one has promised to uphold the same oath of office. But there have been many differences among them. Each man has put his own mark upon the presidency. Some were strong presidents, others were weak. Every decision and action that was made by each of our presidents changed our nation—and often our world—in some way.

This book describes how the office of the presidency has grown and changed since 1789. It examines the role of the president and takes a look at a typical day in the life of our chief executive.

5

WHAT IS THE PRESIDENCY?

The president of the United States heads the executive branch of our government. It consists of three parts: the Executive Office of the president, the Cabinet, and a number of independent agencies. In addition to running the executive branch, the president has many other responsibilities.

The Executive Office of the President

How would you like to have almost two thousand people working for you? That's about how many employees make up the Executive Office. That number includes everyone from secretaries to assistants who function as the president's closest advisers. They work directly for the president, who also holds the title of chief executive.

Opposite: **Thousands of people gather on Capitol Hill to see Bill Clinton sworn in as America's forty-second president.**

Also part of the Executive Office are many different agencies that advise the president. The most important one is the National Security Council (NSC). The NSC supervises our intelligence and defense agencies. The Office of Management and Budget (OMB) prepares the federal budget, which the president submits to Congress each year. Other agencies in the Executive Office are the Council of Economic Advisers, Council on Environmental Quality, Office of Policy Development, Office of Science and Technology Policy, Office of Administration, Office of the United States Trade Representative, and Office of the Vice President.

The Roles of the President

Article II of the Constitution gave the president the power to make treaties and appoint public officials. The president was also named commander-in-chief of the armed forces. Through the years, Congress and the court system have added to these duties. Powerful presidents have also taken on additional functions. Today, the presidency includes seven main roles, which are outlined as follows:

Chief Executive

As chief executive, the president must make sure that all laws and court rulings are obeyed. Under the Constitution, the chief executive was given the power to appoint all officials in the executive branch. Later, legislation gave the president the power to prepare budgets and reorganize agencies. Today, the president is in charge of more than three million federal employees, such as postal clerks, park rangers, and customs officials. Since the chief executive cannot work with each employee, he appoints supervisors to make sure day-to-day operations run smoothly.

Head of State

As our nation's chief of state, the president represents all Americans. His office is the symbol of the citizens, laws, and government of the United States of America. The president maintains relationships with leaders from other countries. He gives out awards to athletes, outstanding students, and other Americans who have excelled. He also attends historical celebrations. Many presidents have enjoyed the privilege of throwing out the first ball at the start of the baseball season.

Commander-in-Chief

As leader of our armed forces, the president constantly makes important decisions about defense and national security. He can both appoint generals and remove them from their positions.

President Franklin D. Roosevelt (seated) signs the declaration of war against Japan in December 1941.

President Harry S. Truman tells news reporters about Japan's surrender at the end of World War II. Truman made a historic decision to drop the atomic bomb on Hiroshima, which ultimately led to Japan's surrender.

Although only Congress can declare war, the president must oversee all our military actions. On occasion, our commander-in-chief has sent American troops overseas to fight, even without a declaration of war, in situations such as the Korean War (1950–1953) and the Vietnam War (1957–1975). In addition, the president alone is responsible for making the decision whether or not to use nuclear weapons in battle.

Chief Diplomat

Under the Constitution, the president was given the power to make treaties and appoint ambassadors, as long as the Senate gives its approval. This role has grown and now requires that the president also set

American foreign policy. He determines the standards by which the United States will treat other countries. The president is also responsible for deciding whether or not to recognize the formation of a new nation.

A number of modern presidents have assumed the challenging role of world peacemaker. Some have sent American soldiers abroad to help keep the peace in warring nations. They have also met with foreign leaders to help find peaceful solutions to difficult conflicts. For example, President Theodore Roosevelt helped to end the Russo-Japanese War (1904–1905). For his admirable contributions, he became the first American to win the Nobel Peace Prize.

In 1979, President Jimmy Carter successfully worked to help Israeli Prime Minister Menachem Begin (right) and Egyptian President Anwar Sadat (left) reach a peace agreement between their countries.

Legislative Leader

The president does not have the power to pass laws. That is the job of Congress. But he can recommend legislation. At the start of each congressional session, the president gives a State of the Union address. In this speech, he describes the bills that he would like to have passed by Congress. The longest State of the Union address ever given was by Harry S. Truman in 1946—it was 25,000 words long!

Party Leader

Since the rise of different political parties (groups of people organized for the purpose of directing the policies of the government), the president has taken over the role of the leader for the party to which he belongs. He helps decide its platform, which describes what the party's positions are on a variety of important issues. The president endorses, or supports, all the campaigns of his party members and may appoint faithful party members to some government positions.

President Franklin D. Roosevelt delivers a State of the Union address to Congress on January 6, 1941.

THE CABINET AND INDEPENDENT AGENCIES

The president's Cabinet is made up of the vice president and fourteen heads of the executive departments. These departments are as follows: State, Treasury, Defense, Justice, the Interior, Agriculture, Commerce, Labor, Health and Human Services, Housing and Urban Development, Transportation, Energy, Education, and Veterans Affairs.

Cabinet members are chosen by the president for their experience and knowledge in their fields. No votes are taken at Cabinet meetings. The members' roles are to offer advice to the president and oversee their particular departments. All Cabinet members must be approved by the Senate before they are allowed to serve.

The Cabinet has not always had fifteen members. As our country has grown, its needs have changed. New executive departments have been formed and old ones have been combined.

In addition to the Cabinet, there are also more than two hundred different independent agencies that make up the executive branch. They administer government programs in a wide variety of areas, such as banking, communications, nuclear energy, labor relations, and veterans' affairs. These agencies include the National Aeronautics and Space Administration (NASA), the Small Business Administration, the Federal Trade Commission, and the United States Postal Service.

National Leader

Beginning with George Washington, each American president has put our nation's interests first. The president tries to make decisions that are based on what would be best for the country, and promotes American business and American products. Abroad, the president shares our ideals and beliefs with the rest of the world.

13

RUNNING FOR OFFICE

Some people say that "anyone can be president." But in addition to the presidency being one of the most difficult jobs in the country, there are also rules about who is eligible. According to the Constitution, the president must be at least thirty-five years of age and a natural-born citizen of the United States. The president must also have lived in the United States for at least fourteen years.

The president serves a four-year term and may only be re-elected once (as stated in the Twenty-second Amendment of 1951). He earns $200,000 per year and receives an additional $50,000 for expenses. The president also receives funds for an office staff, office space, and postage.

Opposite: **Delegates at the Democratic Convention in July 1992 show their support for presidential and vice-presidential nominees Bill Clinton and Al Gore.**

15

So far, all of our presidents have been white males. Only one, John F. Kennedy, has been Roman Catholic. They have all been at least forty-two years old. But there is nothing in the Constitution that limits the office to these characteristics. As more women and minorities are elected to public office, chances are that one of them will be elected president or vice president of the United States.

Woodrow Wilson (standing inside the car) campaigning for re-election in 1917.

Electing a President

Americans hold a variety of ideas about how our government should be run. They form political parties with other people who hold similar views. Each party nominates (proposes) its own candidate for president. The largest political parties, the Democrats and the Republicans, select their presidential candidates during national conventions. These conventions, which are broadcast on television, spread the excitement of the election process across the entire country.

After the candidates are nominated, the election campaign starts. In recent years, candidates have needed to raise millions of dollars to cover campaign costs. They and their families travel around the country, giving speeches about their views on major issues and meeting voters. The major candidates debate these issues on television.

Rutherford B. Hayes was America's nineteenth president.

Election Day

Voters cast their ballots (register their votes) on the first Tuesday following the first Monday in November. This is known as the popular vote. Television broadcasters declare a winner after the popular vote has been counted. But the popular vote does not actually elect the president. This is done the following December during meetings of the Electoral College. The Electoral College is made up of electors—people chosen by voters of each state to elect the president and vice president of the United States. Each state has the same number of electors as it does senators and representatives. (The District of Columbia, which has no senators or representatives, has three electors.) Each state's electors are pledged to vote for the candidate that won the popular vote in that state. Whichever candidate gets the most electoral votes wins the presidency.

In the past, the winner of the popular vote has also won the electoral vote all but two times. In 1876, Rutherford B. Hayes, and in 1888, Benjamin Harrison, were elected with a majority of the electoral votes although their opponents had more popular votes.

Inauguration Day

On January 20 following an election, the president is inaugurated, or takes office. He takes the official oath of office and gives the inaugural address, or speech. Then the president and First Lady either drive or walk down Pennsylvania Avenue in the inaugural parade.

Other Routes to the Presidency

In addition to being elected, there are several other ways of becoming president of the United States. These procedures are spelled out in Article II of the Constitution, the Twelfth, Twentieth, and the Twenty-fifth amendments, and the Presidential Succession Act.

Article II of the Constitution

There have been nine times in history that the vice president has stepped in to finish a president's term. Each time the process was orderly, because Article II of the Constitution had already established the entire procedure. This article states that when the president dies in office, resigns, is removed from office, or cannot fulfill the duties of president, the vice president takes over the position.

THE OATH OF OFFICE

At noon on January 20 of the year following a presidential election, our new president repeats this oath of office:

"I do solemnly swear (or affirm) that I will faithfully execute the Office of President of the United States, and will to the best of my ability, preserve, protect and defend the Constitution of the United States."

The Constitution does not specifically state where the oath of office is to be taken. George Washington was sworn in once in New York City, and once in Philadelphia. After the death of President William McKinley, Theodore Roosevelt took the oath of office in Buffalo, New York. Lyndon B. Johnson is the only president who was actually sworn in on an airplane. He took the oath of office aboard *Air Force One* at Love Field in Dallas, Texas, after President John F. Kennedy had been shot in 1963.

Eight vice presidents have completed the terms of presidents who have died. The vice presidents were: John Tyler, Millard Fillmore, Andrew Johnson, Chester A. Arthur, Theodore Roosevelt, Calvin Coolidge, Harry S. Truman, and Lyndon B. Johnson. Gerald R. Ford became president when Richard M. Nixon resigned.

What would happen if none of the candidates won a majority of the electoral votes or there was a tie? Under Article II of the Constitution, the House of Representatives would select the president. Each state casts one vote. This situation has taken place twice. The House picked Thomas Jefferson to be president in 1801, and John Quincy Adams in 1825.

Vice President Gerald R. Ford became America's thirty-eighth president in 1974, following the resignation of Richard M. Nixon.

The Presidential Succession Act

The Presidential Succession Act would go into effect if both the president and vice president died or left office during their term. In this instance, the next person in line to become president would be the Speaker of the

Our first vice president, John Adams, said that his office was "the most insignificant" ever invented.

The first Congress set the vice president's salary at only $5,000, compared to $25,000 for the president. In the Constitution, they gave only one duty to the vice president: presiding over the Senate.

In the beginning of America's history, there were no separate elections for president and vice president. The person with the most votes became president and chief executive. The one with the second-highest total was vice president.

This system worked well in the first two elections, when both candidates were from the same party. But in 1796, John Adams, a Federalist, was elected president. Then Thomas Jefferson, who was the presidential candidate of the Democratic-Republican Party, became vice president. They did not work well together. Beginning in 1804, the Twelfth Amendment set separate elections for the two offices.

Beginning in 1921, the vice president has been invited to attend Cabinet meetings. Since 1949, the vice president has been a member of the National Security Council, which makes decisions on foreign policy and defense issues.

The modern vice presidency is very different from the role John Adams played. The "veep" has three different offices and often works fourteen hours a day. Since 1974, the vice president has lived in an official residence, a mansion in Washington, D.C.

The vice president is said to be only a heartbeat away from becoming president of the United States. Although Vice President John Adams called his office "insignificant," he knew it was important. He said, "In this I am nothing. But I could be everything."

House, followed by the president pro tempore of the Senate. The next people who would be in order to take these positions would be the members of the Cabinet, beginning with the secretary of state. To date, this act has never been used.

DAILY LIFE OF THE PRESIDENT

The president of the United States lives and works at the White House located on Pennsylvania Avenue in Washington, D.C. The large, 132-room mansion is surrounded by 18 acres of parkland. The grounds are maintained by the National Park Service.

The president works in the Oval Office on the main floor. The family's living quarters are on the second floor. Almost anything the family needs can be obtained without leaving the White House. There is a physician's office, dental clinic, barbershop, and tailor's shop. The White House also has its own machine shop, carpentry shop, and bomb shelter.

The government provides free telephone service and pays for the electricity, which may be as high as $200,000 per year. But the president must pay for

Opposite:
The Oval Office is the room in the White House in which the president does much of his daily work.

23

certain expenses, such as all the laundry products and shampoo that he and the "First Family" use. He is also responsible for paying for his family's food.

The president gives many parties and receptions. If these events are directly related to government business, the expenses are covered. However, the president must pay for all other parties, receptions, and social functions.

Security

Because of their position, the First Family must give up some of their privacy in exchange for security. Their home is toured by about 30,000 visitors each week. The president can't even step out of his front door without attracting attention. Everywhere they go, the president and his family must be accompanied by Secret Service agents who serve as bodyguards. Agents even check the president's food to make sure it hasn't been poisoned.

Four of our nation's presidents have been killed while serving their term of office. Two of them were Abraham Lincoln (1865) and James Garfield (1891). Following President William McKinley's assassination in 1901, the Secret Service was assigned the duty of protecting all of our presidents. The death of John F. Kennedy in 1963, led to the Secret Service providing protection for the widow and children of a former president, as well. Others, including Harry S. Truman, Gerald R. Ford, and Ronald Reagan, have survived

assassination attempts.

Transporting the President

For maximum safety, the president and his family usually travel by government transportation. More than one dozen limousines and cars are available, as well as a bulletproof railroad car. A marine helicopter is used for nearby destinations. For longer flights, the president uses *Air Force One*. This airplane is a modified 747 that carries eighty passengers plus a crew of twenty-three. Inside, it is divided into sections furnished with desks, sofas, beds, and up-to-date communications equipment.

The president's family and invited guests are allowed to fly on these aircraft. However, they must pay for their flights, unless they are traveling on official government business. The usual rate is first-class commercial airfare plus one dollar.

Air Force One can be used by the president for both official and unofficial trips.

PRESIDENTIAL FACTS

There are hundreds of interesting facts that many people don't know about our presidents.

For instance: The United States first had a vice president before it had a president—John Adams took the oath of office nine days before George Washington was sworn in as president.

Did you know that President Washington held two jobs during the first year of his presidency? In addition to being president, George Washington operated a ferry boat service across the Potomac River.

Our third president, Thomas Jefferson, had a pet mockingbird. It followed him around, rode on his shoulder, and took food from his lips.

Abraham Lincoln is the only president to have been granted a patent on an invention. U.S. Patent No. 6,469 is for a hydraulic device that lifts ships up and over sandbars and shoals (shallow spots).

Ulysses S. Grant established the first national park—Yellowstone. Grant's daughter, Nellie, was born on the Fourth of July. As a child, she thought the fireworks on that day were in honor of her birthday.

The first president to have a telephone in the White House was Rutherford B. Hayes. His wife, Lucy, started the custom of egg-rolling on the White House lawn at Easter.

James Garfield could write with both hands—at the same time. He wrote Latin with one hand and Greek with the other.

Only one president, Grover Cleveland, served two separate terms. The "Baby Ruth" candy bar was named after Cleveland's older daughter, Ruth.

The teddy bear was named after Theodore "Teddy" Roosevelt. He was the first president to ride in a car, travel in a submarine, and visit a foreign country while in office.

Woodrow Wilson played golf in the snow on the White House lawn. He painted the golf balls black so he could see them. His second wife, Edith, learned to ride a bicycle—up and down the White House halls.

Rest and Recreation

For relaxation, the White House has a heated pool, a one-lane bowling alley, a small gym, a tennis court, and a movie theater. Every president since Franklin Delano Roosevelt has also had use of Camp David, a retreat in the mountains of Maryland. It is only thirty minutes away from Washington, D.C., by helicopter. Yet, it is secluded and private. A chain-link fence topped by barbed wire keeps away unwanted visitors. Within the compound are a swimming pool, bowling alley, tennis court, riding stable, and archery range. Camp David is one of the few places in the United States where our chief executive can step outside for a private walk.

A Day in the Life

Until about 1930, the president had a light workload. In 1905, Teddy Roosevelt worked in the morning, exercised all afternoon, and read in the evenings. Most Americans didn't seem to mind. They didn't expect the president or the government to be heavily involved in their lives.

With the coming of the Great Depression and World War II, however, the situation changed. The government was expected to do more to help its citizens. Because the president was the leader of the government, he, too, was expected to do more. Dwight D. Eisenhower was criticized for playing too much golf. By this time, Americans expected the presidency to be a full-time job.

Dwight D. Eisenhower was an army general before serving our nation as its thirty-fourth president.

Bill, Hillary, and Chelsea Clinton often do things together as a family when their hectic schedules allow.

President Bill Clinton keeps a busy schedule, often working late into the night or on weekends. Most mornings he and his wife, Hillary Rodham Clinton, are up by 6 A.M. The president likes to drink a cup of coffee in the private family kitchen on the second floor of the White House. He visits with his teenaged daughter, Chelsea, as she gets ready for school. Before he became president, Bill Clinton used to drive Chelsea to school. Now a chauffeur drives Chelsea to the private school she attends in Washington, D.C.

Some mornings the president jogs before beginning his busy workday. A typical day might include meetings with members of Congress, the Cabinet, and Vice President Gore. Other important tasks are signing legislation and reading reports. Staff members may present briefings, which are informational meetings on specific topics.

President Clinton is not the best at keeping to his schedule. He has been known to stretch meetings scheduled for ten minutes into two-hour sessions. But the president's staff members say he's good at dealing with the amount of reading and paperwork that comes across his desk each day.

During each workday, the president spends a lot of time on the telephone. He talks to congressional leaders and with his staff members. He usually talks to Hillary at least three or four times a day. They might discuss the new health care plan or several other government programs. Of course, they often chat about their daughter.

Family time is very important to the president. He tries to arrange his schedule to have dinner with Chelsea and Hillary every night at about 7 P.M. He enjoys watching movies and basketball games with Chelsea. Sometimes they play card games such as crazy eights. The president also helps his daughter with her math homework. He goes to her soccer and softball games whenever he can.

On some evenings, the president goes back to his office (called the Oval Office) downstairs in the White House. There he makes phone calls, does paperwork, and catches up on his reading. When he works in his office at night, the president often wears casual clothes such as jeans and sneakers.

One of the many tasks in President Clinton's day may be to sign legislation.

On some evenings, the president may attend a special event. For example, he and Hillary may host a White House dinner for foreign leaders.

Since the United States is a world leader, the president's duties sometimes take him abroad. In January 1994, for example, President Clinton met with leaders from Russia, Ukraine, the Czech Republic, and Slovakia. His schedule on one day in Moscow included meeting with President Boris Yeltsin and other Russian leaders. At a dinner in the evening, President Clinton played his saxophone for President

President Clinton entertains a crowd of American soldiers stationed in South Korea in 1993.

Yeltsin and the other guests. The twenty-two-course dinner included many Russian foods including moose lips. All in a day's work!

The White House Office

At the heart of the Executive Office of the President is the White House Office. It is made up of a group of assistants to the president. They may carry out the president's main duties. For example, the president's chief of staff is an expert in working with members of Congress. He listens to their opinions and tries to get them to support many of the president's programs. The president's deputy chief of staff supervises the day-to-day operations of the White House staff.

The counselor to the president gives advice on important issues. He is there to listen when the president needs a "friendly pair of ears," and presents the president's viewpoints to government officials.

The press secretary meets with members of the media and issues press releases that express the president's views and decisions on issues.

Other presidential assistants gather information on important topics. Their reports help the president make decisions about policies both at home and abroad. Still other staffers write speeches and prepare legislative proposals.

The first formal White House staff was proposed by Franklin D. Roosevelt in 1939. Congress approved his request for a six-member staff. Today about four hundred people assist the president.

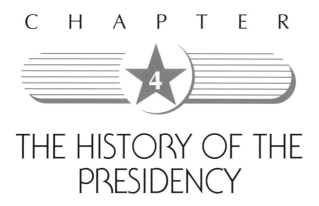

THE HISTORY OF THE PRESIDENCY

When the Revolutionary War ended in 1781, a new set of laws was created. Under the Articles of Confederation, Americans were governed by Congress. The Congress was given only limited powers, such as the ability to declare war. The Articles kept the federal government weak compared to the states. If the new nation was to survive, the federal government needed to be stronger.

In 1787, delegates met in Philadelphia. Instead of changing the Articles, they wrote an entirely new Constitution. Together, the Founding Fathers created a democratic system of government with three branches: legislative, judicial, and executive.

The head of the executive branch would lead the government and be known as "president." The Founding Fathers wanted a strong presidency. But

Opposite: George Washington's inauguration in 1789.

33

In 1787, delegates met in Philadelphia to write laws for the new nation. The Constitution became the foundation of our government today.

they did not want their new leader to be as powerful as a king. They set limits to prevent the abuse of presidential power. The other branches could check, or control, presidential actions. For example, the president nominates Cabinet members and justices of the Supreme Court, but the Senate must approve them.

Impeachment is the strongest method of controlling presidential power. If the president is suspected of wrongdoing, he may be impeached (formally charged with misconduct) by the House of Representatives. Only one president, Andrew Johnson, has been impeached. However, he was acquitted, or ruled not guilty, by the Senate, which always votes on the charges made against a president.

The Beginning of the Role

In 1789, George Washington was unanimously elected our first president. From the very beginning, Washington considered how his actions would shape the role of the presidency. He established many new programs, such as a national bank, and issued national currency.

Thomas Jefferson continued to increase the power of the presidency. In 1803, he approved a treaty to buy the massive Louisiana Territory from France. The Constitution does not specifically state that the chief executive has the power to buy territory. But it does give the president power to make treaties. Therefore, Jefferson decided the Louisiana Purchase was constitutional. This set a tradition for future land purchases.

After President Jefferson left office, Americans began to look differently at the presidency. Prior to this time, only the wealthy and those who owned land were allowed to vote. By 1825, however, the right to vote was no longer tied to owning property. For the first time, candidates began to campaign among the people.

Andrew Jackson profited from these changes. He was a self-educated man who felt strongly that he represented all the people of the nation. He used the veto (the power of a president to reject a bill, or a proposed law) to block any bills that he did not like. Previous presidents had vetoed only legislation that they thought was unconstitutional.

Thomas Jefferson became our third president in 1801.

The Civil War was a time of great turmoil for the office of the presidency.

Power in Wartime

Whenever America has gone to war, the president has assumed additional power. That was the case during the Civil War (1861–1865). It was a conflict between the Union (northern states) and the Confederacy (southern states), mainly over ownership of slaves.

Thirty-nine days after Abraham Lincoln was inaugurated, the Civil War began. During the first weeks of the war, he added 75,000 soldiers to the army and navy and released $2 million in federal funds to purchase war supplies. Lincoln felt these actions were necessary to protect the Union.

After Lincoln was assassinated, Vice President Andrew Johnson became president. Johnson felt he had the power to dismiss advisers from office, but Congress disagreed. When Johnson dismissed Secretary of War Edwin M. Stanton, the House of Representatives impeached him for "high crimes and misdemeanors." But on May 16, 1868, the Senate, by one vote, did not convict him.

World Leadership

In the late 1800s and early 1900s, the United States became a world leader. The power and prestige of the presidency greatly increased under presidents such as Theodore Roosevelt. Roosevelt sent troops to protect American interests in Guam, Puerto Rico, and the Philippines. He also cautioned European nations to stay out of Latin American affairs.

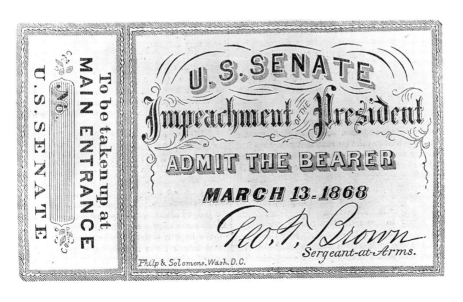

This ticket was for admission to the Senate chamber to witness the impeachment trial of Andrew Johnson.

37

THE FIRST LADY

Martha Washington

So far, all of our presidents have been men. But the president's wife holds an important position.

At first, the role of the president's wife was not clear. Martha Washington acted as a hostess but was not involved in government affairs. Her successor, Abigail Adams, was so interested in politics that some people called her "Mrs. President."

In 1902, Edith Carow Roosevelt was the first to hire a social secretary to keep up with the increasing demands on her time. Edith Bolling Wilson, President Wilson's second wife, decided which officials and papers the president could see after he suffered a stroke in 1919. As a result, critics called her the "Secret President."

Under Eleanor Roosevelt, the role of First Lady grew. Her husband, Franklin Delano Roosevelt, was crippled by polio. Mrs. Roosevelt became his "eyes and ears," traveling the country on fact-finding missions. She held press conferences (to which only women reporters were invited) and expressed her opinions in "My Day," her daily newspaper column.

Some recent first ladies have taken on official roles in political affairs. In 1977, Rosalynn Carter traveled to seven Latin American countries as the president's representative. She was also the first president's wife to attend Cabinet meetings. President Bill Clinton appointed his wife, Hillary Rodham Clinton, to lead the committee in charge of developing a new national health care plan.

It has become a tradition for the First Lady to focus on a special cause or project. Lady Bird Johnson worked to beautify America's highways. Betty Ford supported the arts and improved women's rights. Nancy Reagan waged a war on drug abuse, while Barbara Bush selected literacy as her cause.

The role of First Lady has grown and changed, just as our country has. Each president's wife has shaped the role to fit her talents. Someday we may have a female president. What challenges will face the nation's "First Gentleman?"

On the home front, President Roosevelt encouraged a strong sense of national purpose and patriotism by making many speeches to the American public. He wanted large companies to practice business fairly and honestly. A sportsman and hunter, Roosevelt created more than 125 million acres of national forest land.

As president, Woodrow Wilson was able to help during another time of crisis, World War I (1914–1918). Congress gave him the authority to supervise the military draft and to take control of the railroads, telephone, telegraph, and cable companies.

Theodore Roosevelt became our nation's twenty-sixth president in 1901.

The president who had the most influence on the office was Franklin Delano Roosevelt. FDR took office during the worst economic situation in our nation's history, the Great Depression. Millions of people were out of work. Stores, factories, and banks closed because few people had money to spend or save. Many families lost their farms and homes.

Americans looked to their government—and their president—to pull them out of this terrible economic crisis. FDR acted boldly with a plan that was called the New Deal, which established welfare, Social Security, and the minimum wage. Through New Deal programs, thousands of jobs were created.

A second crisis struck Franklin Roosevelt's administration when World War II began in 1939. FDR held the first peacetime draft (selecting people for duty who are legally required to cooperate) and authorized military assistance to Great Britain.

Part of the reason FDR's presidency became so powerful was that he broke with tradition. He was the only president to serve more than two terms. As a result of this, Congress passed the Twenty-second Amendment to the Constitution in 1951. This amendment restricted presidents to two terms in office.

John F. Kennedy (JFK) was only in office thirty-four months. His impact on the power of the presidency was limited. However, he and his young wife and children brought a sense of new hope and openness to the White House. When Kennedy was assassinated, many Americans felt as if they had experienced a death in the family.

A political cartoon shows FDR on his way to a third term. His vice president, John Garner, was apparently unhappy about this situation.

The seal of our chief executive contains the presidential coat of arms surrounded by fifty stars. This is encircled by the words "Seal of the President of the United States." It includes a bald eagle, our national bird. In one talon, the eagle is holding an olive branch, that stands for peace. In the other talon, the eagle has a bundle of thirteen arrows. In his beak is a gray scroll that reads *E Pluribus Unum* ("Out of many, one"). This motto appears on many official United States items.

The eagle that is on the coat of arms used to face to its left. However, President Harry S. Truman had the seal redesigned so that the eagle would face to its right. This is the traditional direction that represents a show of honor on coats of arms.

The first official flag of the president of the United States was adopted on May 29, 1916. It displayed a president's seal in bronze on a blue background with a white star in each corner. In 1945, President Truman increased the number of stars to forty-eight, one for each state at the time. President Eisenhower added stars for Alaska and Hawaii when they became states.

The president is honored with a twenty-one-gun salute. Tradition says that the salute represents the year 1776, when America declared independence. For this reason, salutes are often fired in this manner: one-seven-seven-six.

Conflict and Criticism

Toward the end of the Vietnam War, the presidency lost prestige. Several crises took place during the administrations of Lyndon B. Johnson and Richard M. Nixon. In the late 1960s and early 1970s, first Johnson and then Nixon sent thousands of troops to

Vietnam without congressional approval. Opposition to the war grew. Americans believed that Johnson and Nixon had both overstepped their powers. They had kept information about the war from Congress. Criticism of Johnson was so strong that he decided not to run for a second term.

Another crisis destroyed the career of President Nixon. On June 17, 1972, five men were arrested for breaking into the headquarters of the Democratic National Committee at the Watergate apartment and office complex in Washington, D.C. The men had planted telephone bugging devices and photographed the office. They worked for President Nixon's re-election committee but would not admit it. Chief aides to the president tried to cover up the situation. By the end of 1973, investigators revealed that Nixon's aides had committed other burglaries and accepted illegal campaign contributions.

On July 27, 1974, the House Judiciary Committee recommended that the full House impeach the president on three charges. These charges were obstruction of justice, abuse of presidential power, and refusal to obey congressional subpoenas (official documents ordering a person to appear in a court of law). Nixon resigned on August 9, 1974, before any action could be taken.

That same day, Vice President Gerald R. Ford became our thirty-eighth president. He was faced with the challenge of rebuilding America's trust in the presidency.

Where Are We Headed?

In the 1980s, during Ronald Reagan's presidency, government involvement in American's lives became more limited. Reagan cut back assistance programs, such as welfare. He also restored some of America's pride in the presidency. The economy expanded and relations with what was then the Soviet Union improved.

Confidence was high during the first part of George Bush's administration. He was careful to get congressional permission before sending troops to the Persian Gulf in 1991. Most Americans felt pride in the success of the Gulf War battles. But as Bush's term

Richard M. Nixon waves goodbye to his staff after resigning from the presidency in August 1974.

43

continued, he seemed more interested in foreign affairs than solving problems at home, such as the weak economy. Americans lost confidence in him and his office, and when his term was over they elected Bill Clinton.

The power of the presidency depends on both the personality of the president and the opinions of the people. How powerful do Americans want a president to be? It seems to depend on the situation. Most Americans want a president they can trust, someone who will represent them well. In crisis situations, such as war, Americans have shown they want a strong leader they can depend on, someone who "stands up" for America.

Presidents of the United States

PRESIDENT	BIRTH	PARTY	TERM	DEATH
George Washington	February 22, 1732; Westmoreland County, VA	Federalist	April 30,1789– March 4, 1797	December 14, 1799; Mt. Vernon, VA
John Adams	October 30, 1735; Braintree (now Quincy), MA	Federalist	March 4, 1797– March 4, 1801	July 4, 1826; Quincy, MA
Thomas Jefferson	April 13, 1743; Albemarle County, VA	Democratic-Republican	March 4, 1801– March 4, 1809	July, 4 1826; Charlottesville, VA
James Madison	March 16, 1751; Port Conway, VA	Democratic-Republican	March 4, 1809– March 4, 1817	June 28, 1836; Orange County, VA
James Monroe	April 28, 1785; Westmoreland County,VA	Democratic-Republican	March 4, 1817– March 4, 1825	July 4, 1831; New York, NY
John Quincy Adams	July 11, 1767; Braintree (now Quincy), MA	Democratic-Republican	March 4, 1825– March 4, 1829	February 23, 1848; Washington, D.C.
Andrew Jackson	March 15, 1767; Waxhaw, SC	Democratic	March 4, 1829– March 4, 1837	June 8, 1845; Nashville, TN
Martin Van Buren	December 5, 1782; Kinderhook, NY	Democratic	March 4, 1837– March 4, 1841	July 24, 1862; Kinderhook, NY
William Harrison	February 9, 1773; Berkeley, VA	Whig	March 4, 1841– April 4, 1841	April 4, 1841; Washington, D.C.
John Tyler	March 29, 1790; Charles City County, VA	Whig	April 4, 1841– March 4, 1845	January 18, 1862; Richmond, VA
James Polk	November 2, 1795; Mecklenburg County, NC	Democratic	March 4, 1845– March 4, 1849	June 15, 1849; Nashville, TN
Zachary Taylor	November 24, 1784; Orange County, VA	Whig	March 4, 1849– July 9, 1850	July 9, 1850; Washington, D.C.
Millard Fillmore	January 7, 1800; Locke, NY	Whig	July 9, 1850– March 4, 1853	March 8, 1874; Buffalo, NY
Franklin Pierce	November 23, 1804; Hillsborough County, NH	Democratic	March 4, 1853– March 4, 1857	October 8, 1869; Concord, NH
James Buchanan	April 23, 1791; Stony Batter, PA	Democratic	March 4, 1857– March 4, 1961	June 1, 1868; Lancaster, PA
Abraham Lincoln	February 12, 1809; Hardin County, KY	Republican	March 4, 1861– April 15, 1865	April 15, 1865; Washington, D.C.

PRESIDENT	BIRTH	PARTY	TERM	DEATH
Andrew Johnson	December 29, 1808; Raleigh, NC	Democratic	April 15, 1865– March 4, 1869	July 31, 1875; Carter Station, TN
Ulysses S. Grant	April 27, 1822; Point Pleasant, OH	Republican	March 4, 1869– March 4, 1877	July 23, 1885; Mount McGregor, NY
Rutherford B. Hayes	October 4, 1822; Delaware, OH	Republican	March 4, 1877– March 4, 1881	January 17, 1893; Fremont, OH
James Garfield	November 19, 1831; Orange, OH	Republican	March 4, 1881– September 19, 1881	September, 19, 1881; Elberon, NJ
Chester Arthur	October 5, 1830; Fairfield, VT	Republican	September 20, 1881– March 4, 1885	November 18, 1886; New York, NY
Grover Cleveland	March 18, 1837; Caldwell, NJ	Democratic	March 4, 1885– March 4, 1889; March 4, 1893– March 4, 1897	June 24, 1908; Princeton, NJ
Benjamin Harrison	August 20, 1833; North Bend, OH	Republican	March 4, 1889– March 4, 1893	March 13, 1901; Indianapolis, IN
William McKinley	January 29, 1843; Niles, OH	Republican	March 4, 1897– September 14, 1901	September 14, 1901; Buffalo, NY
Theodore Roosevelt	October 27, 1858; New York , NY	Republican	September 14, 1901– March 4, 1909	January 6, 1919; Oyster Bay, NY
William Taft	September 15, 1857; Cincinnati, OH	Republican	March 4, 1909– March 4, 1913	March 8, 1931; Washington, D.C.
Woodrow Wilson	December 28, 1856; Staunton, VA	Democratic	March 4, 1913– March 4, 1921	February 3, 1924; Washington, D.C.
Warren Harding	November 2, 1856 Corsica, OH	Republican	March 4, 1921– August 2, 1923	August 2, 1923; San Francisco, CA
Calvin Coolidge	July 4, 1872; Plymouth Notch, VT	Republican	August 3, 1923– March 4, 1929	January 5, 1933; Plymouth, VT
Herbert Hoover	August 10, 1874; West Branch, IA	Republican	March 4, 1929– March 4, 1933	October 20, 1964; New York, NY
Franklin D. Roosevelt	January 30, 1882; Hyde Park, NY	Democratic	March 4, 1933– April 12, 1945	April 12, 1945; Warm Springs, GA
Harry S. Truman	May 8, 1884; Lamar, MO	Democratic	April 12, 1945– January 20, 1953	December 26, 1972; Kansas City, MO
Dwight D. Eisenhower	October 14, 1890; Denison, TX	Republican	January 20, 1953– January 20, 1961	March 28, 1969; Washington, D.C.
John F. Kennedy	May 29, 1917; Brookline, MA	Democratic	January 20, 1961– November 22, 1963	November 22, 1963; Dallas, TX
Lyndon B. Johnson	August 27, 1908; Stonewall, TX	Democratic	November 22, 1963– January 20, 1969	January 22, 1973; San Antonio, TX

PRESIDENT	BIRTH	PARTY	TERM	DEATH
Richard M. Nixon	January 9, 1913; Yorba Linda, CA	Republican	January 20, 1969– August 9, 1974	April 22, 1994 New York, NY
Gerald R. Ford	July 14, 1913; Omaha, NE	Republican	August 9, 1974– January 20, 1977	
James Carter	October 1, 1924; Plains, GA	Democratic	January 20, 1977– January 20, 1981	
Ronald Reagan	February 6, 1911; Tampico, IL	Republican	January 20, 1981– January 20, 1989	
George Bush	June 12, 1924; Milton, MA	Republican	January 20, 1989– January 20, 1993	
William Clinton	August 19, 1946; Hope, AR	Democratic	January 20, 1993–	

For Further Reading

Blassingame, Wyatt. *The Look-It-Up Book of Presidents.* New York: Random House, 1993.

Johnson, Mary Oates. *The President: America's Leader.* Austin, TX: Raintree Steck-Vaughn, 1993.

Kochmann, Rachel M. *Presidents: Birthplaces, Homes, and Burial Sites.* Detroit Lakes, MN: Midwest Printing, 1993.

Paletta, LuAnn. *The World Almanac of First Ladies.* New York: World Almanac, 1990.

Parker, Nancy Winslow. *The President's Cabinet and How It Grew.* New York: HarperCollins, 1991.

Scriabine, Christine Brendel. *The Presidency.* New York: Chelsea House, 1988.

Seuling, Barbara. *The Last Cow on the White House Lawn and Other Little-Known Facts About the Presidency.* Garden City, NY: Doubleday & Co., Inc., 1978.

Index